painting on
glass

Penny Boylan   PHOTOGRAPHY BY Sandra Lane

LAUREL
GLEN

contents

6   Introduction

8   Getting Started

10   Glass

12   Paints

14   Materials

16   Design

18   Techniques

30   Projects

32   Purple Sponged Glasses

36   Frosted Picture Frames

40   Sgraffito Leaf Vase

44   Hoarfrost Shelf

48   Gilded Incense Holders

52   Green Swirl Table Lamp

56   Geometric Plate

60   Etched Door Panel

64   Pink Striped Vase

68   Dotted Pitcher

72   Spray-etched Mirror

76   Fish Canisters

80   Mosaic Bowl

84   Embedded Votives

88   Circular Glass Tabletop

92   Index

96   Suppliers and Acknowledgments

introduction

The joy of glass painting is that it takes very little time to master the basic techniques, so even if you are a complete beginner, with the help of this book you will soon be able to explore your creative side and quickly produce designs to be proud of.

Painting on glass does not require a large work area; most projects can be undertaken on the kitchen table, and work in progress can be carefully put aside to dry between stages on a tray. The chapter "Getting Started" contains a lot of useful information about the materials, paints, designs, and techniques you will need. As a beginner, you will only need a few items of basic equipment, such as a paintbrush, sponges, scissors, and a utility knife. When I am making something by hand, I often find that more time is spent in preparation than in actually carrying out the work; none of the projects in this book take very long to complete. Before you start, it is very important to make sure the glassware is clean and dust-free inside and out; neither masking tape nor paint will adhere to a dusty surface. Remember to remove all sticky labels: use a solvent such as denatured alcohol or even nail polish remover for glue residues and other stubborn marks or grease. Before investing in a whole range of glass and ceramic paints, read the section on the types of paint to use (see page 12). The production of many new types of acrylics has made glass painting even more popular; the glossy transparency of glass paint is particularly appealing, and it poses different design challenges from painting on an opaque surface. Some brands come in extra-small sizes as testers, which are useful for experimentation. The texture of the paint differs from manufacturer to manufacturer, so test just one sample of your favorite color before selecting the paint for your projects.

Each of the fifteen projects lists the materials and techniques you will be using; step-by-step instructions mean the method is easy to follow, and a picture of the finished project shows just what you are aiming for. You can experiment on glass jars and bottles to get the feel of how the paint works; transparent paint needs a little practice to apply. Personally, I don't mind some air bubbles and streaks, but sometimes you'll need a flatter application, and as a beginner you will need to learn how much or how little paint you should apply. You will gradually come to understand just how long some paints take to become absolutely dry, and you can try out the technique of baking work in a home oven to make the paint more permanent.

The motifs used in the various projects in this book are there for you to use, either as a starting point for your own designs or to adapt in size and scale to suit the glassware you wish to decorate. You could try combining several techniques; for example, with the Fish Canisters (see page 76), you could monoprint the fish and decorate them with embedded beads, or try frosting or etching the shapes and painting on the details. I particularly like the special technique for creating a lovely light and airy look on the Sgraffito Leaf Vase (see page 40).

There are lots of alternative design techniques with which you can experiment—just let your imagination take over. Nothing need ever be wasted—I use my experimental jars for holding all my brushes and pens, and they can look very attractive as votive candle holders for the garden. Whether you start with a single project such as a vase or undertake the challenge of decorating a whole set of glasses, I'm sure you'll find painting on glass a highly creative and satisfying pastime.

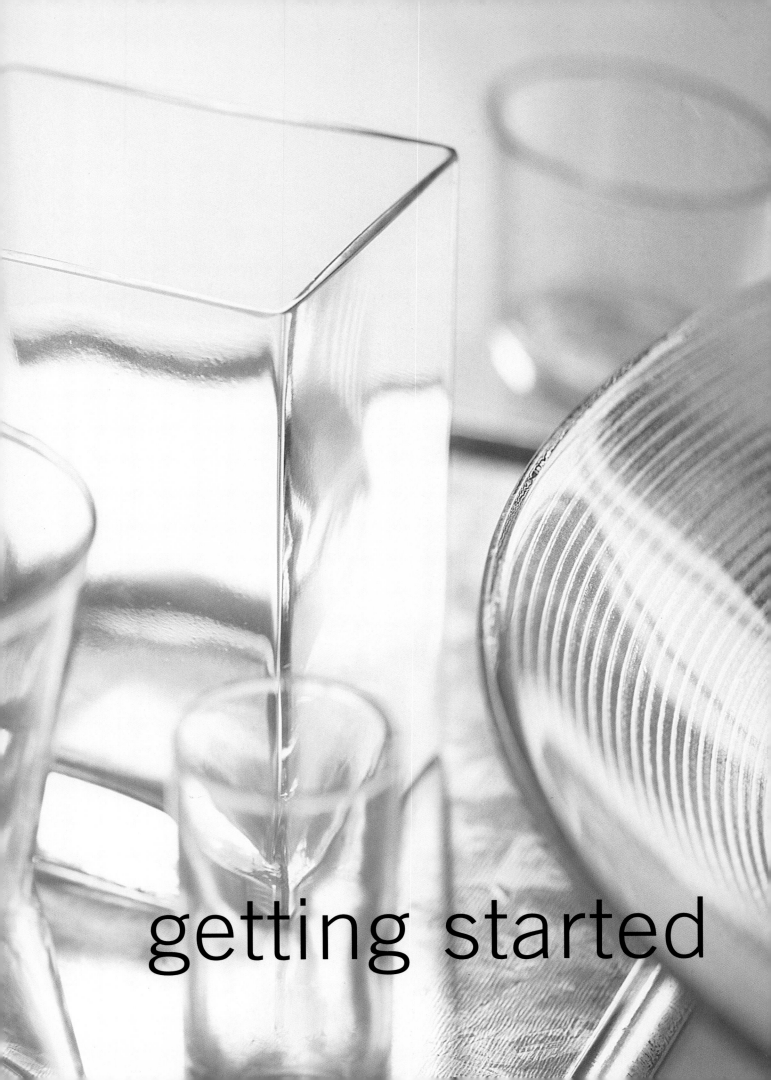

getting started

glass

Painting on glass should not be an expensive pastime; machine-made glass is cheap and widely available, and usually benefits from the addition of some extra decoration. I believe that you shouldn't buy costly pieces for decorating; an expensive item should not need further embellishment with glass paints.

There are countless shapes and sizes of vases, drinking glasses, bottles, and pitchers as well as more unusual items such as plates, dishes, and bowls. You can even successfully decorate interior fixtures; try the Etched Door Panel (page 60), the Hoarfrost Shelf (which give a bathroom an instant lift, see page 144) or the Spray-etched Mirror (page 72).

Don't restrict yourself to plain pieces—look for glassware with interesting textures (made by pressing in a mold) and for colored glass, which gains another dimension with the addition of transparent paint. Some glass pieces have air bubbles trapped inside, some look crackle-glazed, you can find partially etched pieces, and there are plenty of ordinary household products and foodstuffs that come in unusual or prettily shaped containers.

Decorating glass is a lovely way of making individual objects for the home that specifically suit an interior color scheme or that give a "designer" touch to ordinary household necessities without a high price tag. It also allows you to alter the mood of a room scheme by changing some of the elements quickly and inexpensively, and gives you the satisfaction of having created something unique.

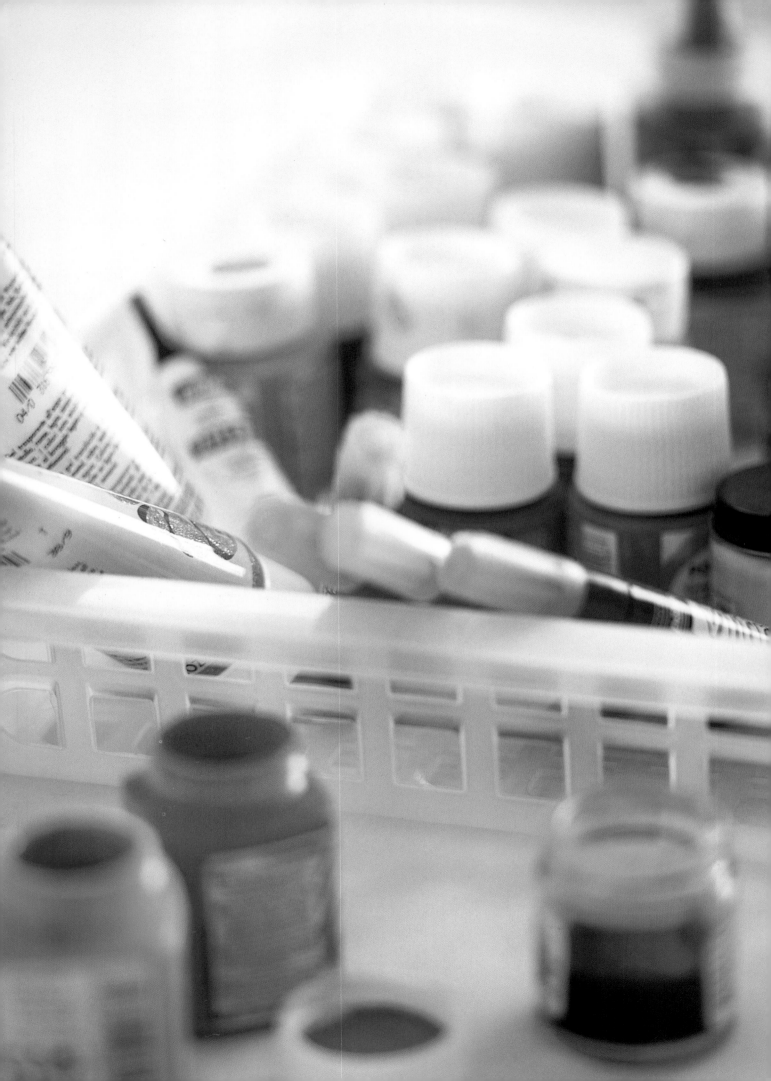

paints

When it comes to buying glass paints, remember that a little goes a long way, and sample sizes are available which you can use to familiarize yourself with the texture and finish of the paint. As a general rule, it is not advisable to mix colors from different suppliers, and you should never mix water-based and solvent-based paints.

Solvent-based paint

This transparent glass paint is air drying and durable, and will withstand gentle washing with liquid detergent and a soft cloth. Colors can be mixed or thinned and varnished for more durability. Brushes can be cleaned with denatured alcohol or paint thinner. Let the paint dry for at least three days.

Water-based paint

This is another transparent glass paint, which can be set by baking, making it durable. (Some manufacturers say items are then dishwasher-safe, but you may not want to take that risk.) Let the paint dry for at least 24 hours before baking. Check the instructions, but generally the item can be placed in a home oven at 325° F for an hour. Do not bake projects that you have embedded with beads or other items that may not be able to withstand heat.

Water-based paints can be intermixed, and there is an exciting selection of auxiliary products such as pearlized medium, colored relief outliner in transparent shades, and felt-tip pens. The pens are useful for drawing the design on the glass prior to painting with the transparent paint, or they can be used on their own for fine, detailed work.

Brushes can be cleaned in water when you want to change colors and, when you are finished with them, given a final clean in soapy water. They differ in texture from solvent-based paints, which are more viscous, and your brushmarks may show more easily.

Ceramic paint

Ceramic paints work just as well as transparent paints, and the water-based versions can also be baked. The opacity of different brands varies considerably. The combination of ceramic and transparent glass paint works exceptionally well with the little fish motifs (see Fish Canisters, page 76) where the ceramic paint acts as a sort of outliner when monoprinted from paper towels onto the glass.

Relief outliner

I have avoided using outliner unless it forms part of the design. It is normally used to contain glass paint and prevent it from running, but it can make motifs look heavy and is not strictly necessary if you work on one section at a time, as with the Sgraffito Leaf Vase (see page 40). Outliner can be used for embedding, and it is available in metallic shades that look lovely with glass beads and pearls.

Gel medium

Gel can appear lumpy when first squeezed from the tube, but this will disappear. The gel can be applied thickly for a three-dimensional effect, but it is heavy and can slide off the glass if the work is not kept flat. It will be touch dry within an hour, but needs a week to dry totally. Brushes can be washed in soapy water. The gel can also be applied with a knife, which can be useful for pushing it into shape or creating a relief texture. It can be baked for extra durability.

materials

A few paintbrushes and masking tape are the most basic materials you will need to invest in to get started; others can be added as you get more familiar with the easier techniques such as sponging and handpainting. You only need to buy specialized items once you would like to start gilding or using etching paste (see suppliers on page 96).

Sponges

Inexpensive man-made sponges for bathroom and kitchen use are the best way of applying paint to large areas of glass. The texture of the sponge will dictate the type of cover you achieve, but generally a close-textured sponge will give the best results. Gently tapping over the same area while the paint is still wet will give the paint a stippled texture and eliminate bubbles, although these are tiny and not a

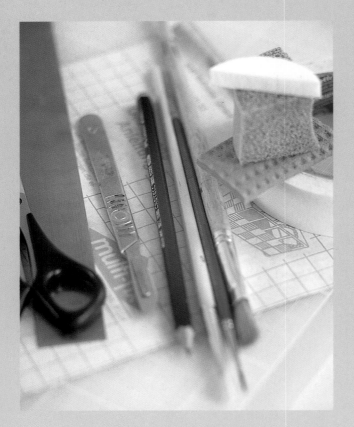

great problem. Do not keep sponging over tacky paint because the whole surface will then become very sticky and will lift off.

Cosmetic sponges, intended for makeup application, and flat kitchen sponges are good for sponging stripes and can also be cut into different shapes for stamping simple motifs (see Purple Sponged Glasses, page 32). The sponges deteriorate quickly, so they should be discarded regularly; it is generally not worth trying to clean them for further applications. If you are not going to be able to complete a project all at once, cut a spare sponge or two so you can finish the work later.

Brushes

The three most useful sizes for the projects are a fine-pointed No. 2 in a man-made fiber and two flat-headed bristle brushes about ¼ inch and ¾ inch wide.

Use the fine-pointed brush for delicate work and for painting motifs where you want the paint to flow onto the glass and settle evenly without drips. Load the brush with paint; then gently touch the tip of the brush to the glass and let the paint flow onto the glass before loading it with any more paint. Avoid stroking the paint on as the brushmarks will show. Practice on some spare glass to get the feel of the particular paint you are using; different brands have thicker or thinner textures.

The bristle brushes give the paint a gentle texture of lines, and they are useful for working in vertical strokes to keep the paint even.

Solvent-based cleaners

Household denatured alcohol will be fine for cleaning solvent-based paints. You can use commercial paint thinners, but they can be quite expensive. After cleaning, always wash the brushes in soapy water to remove the residue.

Masking tape and self-adhesive plastic

Masking tape is the simplest way of attaching templates to the inside of glass objects. It is not totally reliable for masking straight edges since its low-tack properties can allow paint to seep underneath, but that aside, it will work perfectly well if care is taken.

Self-adhesive plastic film is a perfect alternative if you want to make larger cutout stencils. The design can be drawn on the paper backing and then cut out with scissors, a utility knife, or craft knife. The plastic stretches very easily, so be careful when you are applying it to the surface, but this also helps you to squeeze out the air from bubbles and creases. To apply the plastic film, peel off a small area of paper backing and position the plastic before easing off the remaining backing while smoothing it down. Always remove the plastic film soon after the paint is completely dry since it can leave a sticky residue if left for a long period.

design

From sponging to sgraffito, the following techniques will help you create stunning effects on all types of glassware. Each is simple to do, so use them as a starting point to create your own unique designs and motifs.

One of the most important things you should do before you start painting on glass is to practice on well-washed empty jars, bottles, and pots. Not only will you be able to try out different paints for texture and coverage, you can also test your own color mixes and experiment with all the techniques used in this book—all for free.

Consider the purpose of the object you are planning to decorate when deciding which paint to use since durability comes into question if the piece is to be washed frequently or is intended for food use. The size and shape of the glassware will help decide the scale and type of design or motif, whether you want repeat motifs, or just placed designs. To help plan your designs, you will need paper, pencils, a porcelain marker, scissors, and plastic stationery sleeves. Cut out paper templates to stick to the inside of the glass with masking tape, arranging their positions or changing the scale of the motifs until you are happy with the final effect. You may find a porcelain marker useful when you are planning where to put single motifs or drawing lines on the glass. It wipes off easily, but it's best to mark the wrong side of the glass and avoid painting over it since the black will show through transparent paints and cannot then be removed.

Sometimes you will need to experiment in color. Here it is useful to try out the paint on clear plastic, such as stationery sleeves, which can then be cut up

and stuck to the glass with masking tape to give you an even clearer idea of how the balance of color will look. This was the technique used when planning the Geometric Plate (see page 56).

I have studiously avoided the technique of outlining motifs with relief outliner and then filling it in with another paint. This is a matter of taste, but my feeling is that the technique dictates the whole look,

and everything then appears too uniform, or heavy and crude. I prefer the monoprinting technique used for the Fish Canisters (see page 76). Relief outliner is an attractive material in its own right, especially when used in pearlized versions.

Use a photocopier to enlarge or reduce motifs; a change of scale can drastically alter a design, either giving it greater impact or a more subtle approach.

When changing scale, you may need to draw over the motif on tracing paper several times, altering it bit by bit until you have the effect you require.

If you're not confident about designing your own motifs, there are many sources you can consult for ideas. Refer to catalogs, magazines, and books for inspiration, and adapt any designs that appeal to you and to the requirements of your project.

techniques

Having chosen your glass object, considered the available materials and the nature of the design, the next challenge is actually to apply the paints. The following pages explore various painting techniques that can be adapted to suit your chosen designs.

There are some basic procedures and techniques to bear in mind that will give better results when applying paint to glass surfaces. Don't buy expensive palettes for painting on glass, especially since solvent-based paints cannot be washed off. Use the paint straight from the jar or, if you prefer to mix colors, pour a small amount into an old jar lid or a plastic tray. You can cover the receptacle with plastic wrap before adding paint, then change it when you want to change colors.

Using transparent glass paint requires a little practice as runs and drips are common with viscous paint. Load your brush, then touch it to the glass and the paint will flow from the brush, adding paint as you go. It will spread to cover the area, and although you rarely achieve a completely flat cover, the slight differences in tone are part of the attraction.

If the paint runs under a stencil or masking tape or if you make a mistake when painting by hand, it can be scraped off with the blade of a craft knife when it is nearly dry. Mistakes in wet paint should be wiped away with a paper towel wrapped around the pointed end of scissors. If you make a more serious mistake, the paint can be scratched off with a pan scourer under water and given a final cleaning with denatured alcohol to remove any lingering flakes.

Once completed, give the surface a coat of clear varnish to make it more durable. This is useful for protecting gilded surfaces, but always use a clear gloss varnish—a flat finish can dull the surface.

Hand-painted samples

The jars here show experiments with freestyle painting. Try combining transparent with opaque paint or use felt-tip pens to draw the shape before painting for a more delicate effect. You could also cover the transparent paints with a thin layer of pearlized paint when dry and use the felt-tip pens on top of the design to add delicate details.

sponging

This is one of the most versatile techniques used in glass painting. An excellent method for coloring larger areas, it is possible to achieve impressive repeat patterns quickly and easily. All the samples shown in the picture on the left were created using either a household sponge cloth, a cellulose bath sponge, or a fine latex makeup sponge, simply cut to shape with scissors.

1 Sponging the stripes

Cut a piece of cellulose sponge into a long rectangle and then load transparent solvent-based paint on the cut edge using a paintbrush. Don't dip the sponge directly into the paint; this often results in too much paint being soaked up. Gently press the sponge onto the glass to make stripes; you can then work over the areas already sponged if you want to achieve a stronger color.

2 Sponging the checks

Cut a small piece of fine latex makeup sponge into a piece long enough to hold comfortably and trim it on the end to produce a small square shape. Gently load the surface with pink solvent-based paint and sponge onto the glass between the stripes.

Three-dimensional sponging samples

The samples shown opposite are applied to glass jars with fluted edges. Using sample glass objects this way means designs and techniques can be practiced on three-dimensional shapes. Thin pieces of cellulose dishwashing sponge were curved into a roughly circular shape and then anchored in place with masking tape. The sponge was folded in half to create a pleasing all-over design of purple circles. This initial design was then developed with simple sponge stamps made from a latex makeup sponge to create a mosaic tile shape. Finally some of the squares were sponged over once again with a smaller shaped sponge in a complementary color.

gilding

Whether you choose loose metal leaf or transfer leaf, gilding is a simple technique to master and the results are spectacular. It is important to allow the gold size (the adhesive) time to dry sufficiently before you apply the metal leaf. If you try to gild over gold size that is too tacky, the metal leaf breaks off and becomes glued to everything except the glassware. Remember to be patient; the gold size should be only barely moist. If in doubt, leave it a few minutes more. Most manufacturers give guidelines, but it can depend on the conditions you are working in as to how long you will need.

The steps here are shown using transfer metal leaf which, although more expensive than loose metal leaf, is much easier to use and useful for designs where you are planning to use a motif such as those shown on the tall glass bottles.

1 Creating the template
Cut out a template, then transfer the image onto the tracing paper backing of the metal leaf with a pencil. Cut the tissue out carefully with scissors. Place the template under the glass, making sure it is facing in the same direction as the piece of metal leaf that you have cut out.

2 Adding acrylic gilding medium
Paint over the template area with acrylic gilding medium using a No. 2 paintbrush. It can be difficult to see the medium when it has dried, so you can add a tiny amount of watercolor paint to help it show up.

3 Gilding the glassware
Let the adhesive dry, then carefully place the metal leaf shape over the gold size and pat it into place before removing the tissue backing. Varnish with gloss water-based (acrylic) varnish.

Gilding samples

These three tall bottles were used as practice pieces, but they also make a stunning display. The wavy lines give a slightly cleaner edge to the gilding and were done with transfer metal leaf, cut to shape. The spots were painted freestyle in gilding medium, then gilded in both silver and gold metal leaf. The design was built up by painting a few spots and gilding them first before adding to the design. The geometric shapes were created with masking tape, which was removed before applying the silver leaf. When this had dried, the shapes for the gold leaf were painted freestyle.

Monoprinting samples

The motifs here were executed using the same method as the fish skeleton. The nautilus shell uses pearlized outliner, which is a softer color to pick out the swirl outline. The purple shell was monoprinted in outliner before painting and needed no further decoration. The little boat was more suited to a colorful treatment, so the positions of the two colors were reversed on alternate motifs.

monoprinting

This technique is an incredibly effective alternative to using relief outliner to help provide a framework for transparent glass paint, which can be difficult to stop from dripping and running. Using opaque ceramic paint for the print contrasts well with the more delicate transparency of glass paint, but it is also an effective and quick way of applying a repeat motif for an all-over design. Monoprinting does not work well for large areas of paint, so always use a design that works well as line only, such as this fish skeleton.

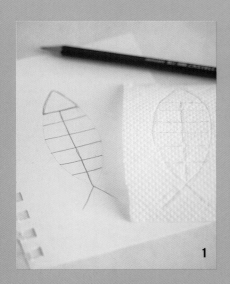

1 Tracing the design

Trace your motif onto a small piece of paper towel using a pencil. There should be a margin of paper measuring about ¼ inch all the way around the image.

2 Painting the outline

Using water-based ceramic paint and a No. 2 paintbrush, paint the outline of the motif. Do not allow the paint to bleed by wetting the brush between applications. Make sure you use quite a lot of paint as it is easily absorbed into the paper towel and you want enough so that it will transfer onto the glass.

3 Transferring the motif

Carefully place the paper face down on the glass and press down over the painted outline only with the blunt end of the paintbrush or the pencil to help transfer the motif. Peel away the paper, leaving the printed motif behind. Any large gaps where the paint has not transferred can be filled in with a paintbrush using a stippling action to imitate the printed texture. Add transparent glass paint to finish the image, or leave the motif just as it is.

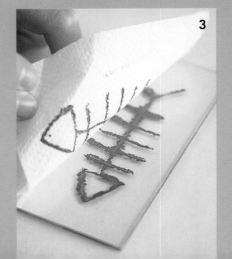

embedding

Another simple technique that is also very versatile. Seed beads are most effective when embedded into the paints; they do not dominate the glass object too much, but add an interesting texture. They can simply be dropped into the wet paint and gently pressed into it. This basic process can be adapted with different colors, and varying the colors, shapes, and finish of beads.

Using transparent water-based glass paint

One method of embedding is to apply transparent water-based glass paint to the glass as the base, so the embedded items are the main focus of the decoration. The paint will look white at first but will eventually dry clear. Then drop glass seed beads into the paint, picking up any stray beads and easing them into the paint with the point of a needle or pin.

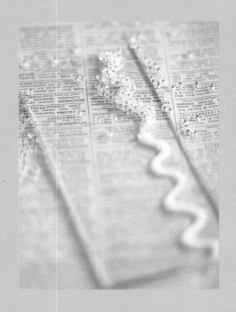

Embedding samples

The white sample glass shown opposite was done on a white pearlized background using a circle of white pearlized outliner in the middle, into which tiny pearl beads were dropped. A thinner line was made around this and long silver bugle beads arranged around it before placing a few more pearls in the gaps. The rim was decorated when the first design had dried. The green sample uses silver outliner, which was applied in a zigzag line, then embedded in a random pattern of bugle beads and tiny antique seed beads. The lilac sample used transparent outliner for ceramic painting. Clear glass seed beads were combined with much larger purple glass beads and dropped into small circular blobs of outliner.

The examples opposite show how delicate and luxurious an effect can be created on glassware by adding beads to paint and outliner. You might choose to take a much bolder approach and embed chunkier items such as mosaic tiles, or experiment with larger ceramic and glass beads or glass jewels for embroidery. Once you have tried the technique, you will naturally come up with other ideas. Embedded items are not meant for heavy use, so when cleaning the work be careful not to dislodge the decoration.

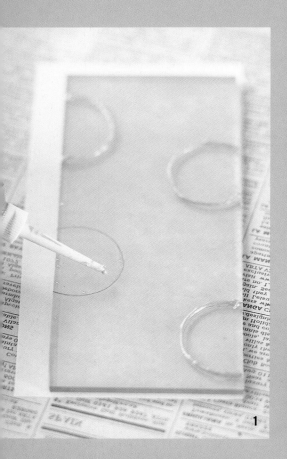

1 Sponging and outlining

Sponge the glass surface all over with pearlized paint and then leave it to dry thoroughly. Put your chosen paper template underneath the glass (attaching it with masking tape for a vessel or three-dimensional form). Then work over the template with the gold outliner to apply a thin line, in this case forming a circle.

2 Placing the beads

While the outliner is still wet, gently put your selection of seed beads into it. Do this by placing the beads on the point of a needle or a pin and dropping them gently into the paint. Finally press them in with the point of the needle or pin to embed them in the paint.

sgraffito

Sgraffito involves scratching away areas of paint in a textural, almost graphic, way. The lines left after the paint has been removed can be quite fine, and work particularly well with the light transparency of glass paints giving an added delicacy to the work.

You can use most basic tools for sgraffito depending on the effect you want. A heavy-gauge sewing needle embedded in a cork is good for detailed lines. Hold the needle close to its point to prevent it from bending as you scratch into the paint. Fine-pointed scissors can be opened a fraction to produce two close parallel points. A small screwdriver and an awl are also worth trying. The type of sgraffito line you achieve also depends on the paint you are using. Some paints become brittle if they are scratched when they are too dry, so test an area on spare glass before embarking on a whole project.

Sgraffito is a useful technique to master if you lack confidence about adding painted detail to your glassware designs. This decorative method also combines well with monoprinted motifs, allowing you to pick out details and patterns without adding further layers of paint. It is also possible to work in sgraffito over gilded decoration, in which case, leave the gilded area to dry thoroughly before scratching away the lines of texture.

etching

Etching paste is available as a thick cream which when applied to glass will create a permanent frosted surface. The cream is applied in a thick layer over a resist stencil cut from self-adhesive plastic using a wide brush, or a small palette knife if you prefer. Wear rubber gloves to protect your skin from the caustic effect of the chemicals and work in a well-ventilated area. Try to achieve an even coverage. The manufacturer's instructions give guidelines on how long to leave the paste before washing it off, but it is always a good idea to have some test pieces coated with paste alongside your project to see if the etching effect is sufficient before washing off. Make sure the stencil used is stuck on very well to the glass or the paste will seep underneath, and mistakes cannot be rectified. Wash the paste off under running water, removing residue with the brush before taking off the stencil, and washing again several times to remove the final residues. It is useful to clean the frosted glass finally with denatured alcohol or solvent-based cleaner to remove greasy fingerprints and watermarks.

projects

These glasses are one of the simplest projects in the book, but the combination of colored glass with a bold motif has a bright, contemporary look. There is no need to use a template for the pattern placement — random sponging all over the glass works well. You can dab the paint in rows or spot-place the motif at random, depending on the size of the glass and the amount of coverage you want to achieve. If you work with water-based paint, you can design the glasses by trial and error, washing off the paint if you are not absolutely happy with the result and trying again until you have created the effect you want. Water-based paint has the added advantage that it can be baked in a very slow oven to make it durable, making it suitable for use on everyday glassware.

Work quickly with the sponges to cover the whole set of glasses at the same time, or make a couple of sponge stamps before you start because they are not very hard-wearing and will become unusable when the paint has dried. This way you will make sure that the patterning on all the glasses is consistent.

purple sponged glasses

you will need

Materials

Colored glasses

Makeup sponges

Scissors for cutting sponges

Craft glue

Transparent glass paint to complement
   color of glass

Techniques

Sponging (see page 20)

Cutting the sponge stamps

Make a sponge stamp by cutting a flat makeup sponge into a square shape, then gluing on a spare piece of sponge to act as a small handle. To make the smaller square of the design, cut another square sponge stamp from the same piece of sponge. This type of sponge is not very durable, so you will need to make enough to complete the project; also it can become a bit overloaded with paint, so keep a piece of old newspaper handy to blot off any excess.

Sponging on the motif

Pour a small amount of transparent glass paint into a container and sponge the glass all over with the larger square motif. Let the paint dry for several hours before stamping a small square in the center of each larger motif, using a darker shade of the same color to achieve a two-tone effect.

Design hint:
• Colored glass looks best sponged in a similar color paint.

Box frames look really stylish and are an inexpensive way of displaying collections of three-dimensional items such as these pebbles. A collection of frames in different shapes and sizes is an instant way to transform a plain mantelpiece.

To give the frames a contemporary feel, they were sponged with frosting medium, which softens the shapes of the pebbles inside.

frosted picture frames

You can buy frosting medium already mixed, and it can also be tinted very slightly with a tiny touch of green to enhance the greenish tinge of the glass itself. The type of sponge you use will affect the texture of the frosting, so use one with a close texture and cut it into a piece that is small enough to hold easily, about 1 inch square.

When you have finished frosting the glass, assemble the frame and put a piece of natural-colored handmade paper on the backing—the perfect texture to display natural objects such as feathers, shells, and driftwood.

you will need

Materials

Picture frame with a very deep surround
   to make into a box frame

Clear self-adhesive plastic

Cutting mat

Craft knife or utility knife

Metal ruler

Masking tape

Clear glass paint

White glass paint

Paintbrush for mixing

Close-textured sponge such as
   a synthetic bath sponge

Techniques

Handpainting

1 Masking the glass

Make a template to mask the section of the glass that is not to be frosted. You can use any shape you want, but if your picture frame has a precut mat, you could use that as a guide. Cut out a piece of self-adhesive plastic using a cutting mat and a metal ruler as a straight edge. Using the grid on the cutting mat as a guide, carefully apply the mask to the glass.

Mixing the frosting medium

In a separate container, mix together transparent paint with a little white paint to make a translucent glaze. Test it on some spare glass such as a glass jar to make sure you have achieved the correct color, but remember that it will dry slightly darker.

2

3

Applying the frosting medium

Load the sponge with frosting medium and apply it to the glass. As is the case with all sponging on larger areas, you will have to go over the same section several times to get an even cover and help eliminate bubbles.

Assembling the frame

When the frosting medium is dry, the box frame can be put together. Make sure you put the plain glass side that has not been sponged on the outside and the frosted side facing in.

The inspiration for the leaf

motif for this vase came from a piece of 1950s fabric. Leaf motifs, or indeed many other natural shapes, are a good inspiration for designs. Keep a small sketchbook to record any motifs that you find attractive—sources could vary from pottery, fabric, and textiles to packaging. The curved shape of this vase was perfect for a random, repeat design, and although curved surfaces

sgraffito leaf vase

are perceived as more difficult to paint on, this is not the case. The secret is to work in sections, leaving the paint to dry sufficiently before turning to work on the next section. A sgraffito technique was chosen to pick out the stylized ribs on the leaf motif to give the whole piece a light and airy feel. The colors were also restricted to only two shades of complementary blue so the vase would not look too busy. If you are working on a curved surface without the use of outliner for the first time, it's a good idea to experiment with the technique on an old glass jar until you are entirely happy with the result.

you will need

Materials

Glass vase

Paper for templates

Pencil

Fine-bladed scissors

Masking tape

No. 2 paintbrush

Cobalt blue and aquamarine paint
   (see Paints, page 12)

Facial tissue

Techniques

Sgraffito (see page 29)

1 Making and positioning templates

Draw a simple leaf template onto paper, scaling it according to the size of your vase. Cut out several blank leaf shapes and attach them to the inside of the vase using small strips of masking tape. Take time to position the leaves at different angles to create a pleasing allover pattern, making sure they are evenly distributed. Stick another small piece of masking tape on the outside of the vase over the leaves you wish to paint in the cobalt blue color, leaving those that will be aquamarine blank. Check that you will achieve a good overall balance of the two colors.

1

Painting on the colors

Begin painting the leaves with a No. 2 paintbrush, using the paper templates as a guide. Rest the base of the vase inside the reel of masking tape at an angle—this will prevent the paint from running and forming drips. You will need to apply quite a lot of paint, loading the brush and then letting the paint flow onto the glass. Only experience will tell you how much to use before the paint runs, but tilting the work while you are painting and letting the paint dry slightly before rotating the vase to work on the next section will help you. Paint all the leaves using the cobalt blue and aquamarine.

Scratching the design

Remove the paper templates and draw the design onto one of them using a dark pencil line. Replace this motif on the inside of the jar against one of the painted leaves using masking tape. Etch this design using a blade of a pair of fine-pointed scissors or a long leather needle stuck into a cork. This technique is most effective if the paint is not completely dry. Brush away the paint flakes as you work with a facial tissue, finally rinsing away any remaining particles in warm soapy water. Let the paint dry completely, or bake the vase in the oven according to the paint manufacturer's instructions.

I used etching paste for this

bathroom shelf since the effect is permanent and will stand up to frequent cleaning. Use frosting medium or glass etch spray if you prefer, especially as the design is worked on the underside of the shelf and seen from the untreated side, to make it easier when cleaning.

The textured design is simple to achieve and is much more stylish than the pressed glass textures often used in bathrooms. This graphic allover pattern is perfect for providing extra privacy when used on a window or shower screen, for example, and you can vary the scale of the design to suit your purposes.

Etching paste is very caustic, so take all the necessary precautions; work in a well-ventilated area and protect all vulnerable surfaces with newspaper. The paste will etch any part of the glass with which it comes into contact, so take great care that none gets on the wrong side of the item. Read the manufacturer's instructions carefully; times will vary for how long you should leave the paste before washing it off, but you can repeat the application if necessary. Check the timing on a spare piece of glass first.

hoarfrost shelf

you will need

Materials

Self-adhesive plastic for masking

Cutting mat

Metal ruler

Craft knife or utility knife

Rubber gloves

Etching paste

Wide, flat-headed ¾-inch brush

Techniques

Etching (see page 29)

1 & 2

1 Cutting the plastic strips

Cut thin strips of self-adhesive plastic long enough to run from edge to edge along the length of the shelf. Work carefully, using the cutting mat, metal ruler, and craft knife or utility knife.

2 Arranging the design

Peel off the backing from each strip and start to lay them on the glass—make sure you are working on the wrong side of the shelf. Work in a random fashion, laying the strips vertically at angles and adding a few strips at angles horizontally. When you have covered the glass and are happy with the design, press all the strips down to make sure the etching paste will not run underneath.

Applying the etching paste

Using rubber gloves to protect your hands, paint a thick layer of etching paste over the entire surface. Avoid gaps and drips at the edges and try to give the shelf a reasonably even coating. Leave the work in a well-ventilated area for at least 20 minutes, or follow the manufacturer's instructions.

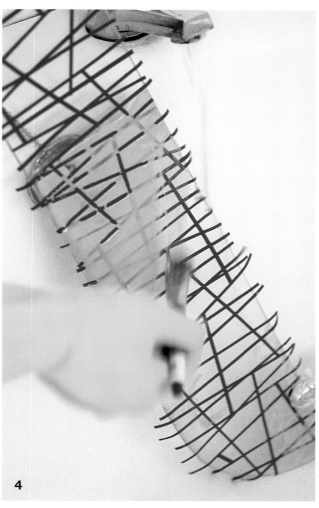

4

3

Revealing the design

Wash off the paste under running water, using the brush to remove any residue. Take care to remove the paste thoroughly, adding some liquid detergent to help if necessary. Dry the glass and remove the plastic masking strips.

Incense creates an intimate

atmosphere in a room in the same way that candlelight does. If they are used together, the overall effect can be quite magical.

Silver metal leaf has a real affinity with glass, and it can be used with great impact on its own without any added color. It is also inexpensive, yet it gives a truly luxurious look to everyday objects. Look for narrow, tall shapes to hold the long incense sticks, such as the vodka shot glasses used here. Fill the glasses with colored sand or use tiny pebbles, which will look pretty and will also ensure that the sticks are anchored safely while they are burning. Three glasses grouped together look more attractive than just one holder on its own—use different colors or the same color for all three. Decide what will suit your chosen room best.

Because of the gilding, this project is unsuitable for glass paint that needs to be baked in the oven to set it. Make sure you use only gloss acrylic varnish to seal the silver leaf since the flat-finish version will dull the sheen, spoiling the final appearance of the incense holders.

gilded incense holders

you will need

Materials

Three tall shot glasses

Pearlized glass or ceramic paint—
  or add pearlized medium to colored
  paint to achieve pearlized effect

Transparent glass paint in colors
  to match the pearlized paints in
  aquamarine, violet, and lime green

Sponge for applying paint

Scissors for cutting sponge

No. 2 paintbrush

Paper for masking

Masking tape

Water-based gold size medium for
  applying the leaf

Two soft paintbrushes—one for applying
  the gold size and one to use dry
  to burnish the silver leaf

Silver metal leaf for gilding

Transparent acrylic gloss varnish

Techniques

Sponging (see page 20)

Gilding (see page 22)

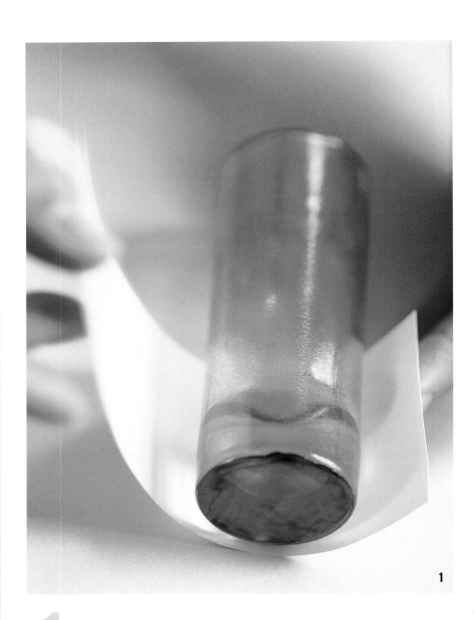

1

Pearlizing the glass

Mix together the pearlized medium with aquamarine paint for the first glass to make pearlized paint, or use ready-made pearlized paint to sponge onto the glass to cover the whole surface completely. Paint the base of the glass with transparent aquamarine paint. This gives the glass more depth of color without having to build up more layers of paint. Let the glass dry completely for at least 48 hours. Now attach a piece of paper around the glass to the height you wish to leave ungilded, securing it with masking tape. Make sure the paper is applied tightly to keep the gold size from seeping underneath.

2 Glazing with gold size

Hold the glass by the paper-covered end and paint on a thin glaze of the gold size. Take care not to let drips form at the lip of the glass and avoid getting the paper mask wet. Let the gold size dry for the time stated in the manufacturer's instructions. It will feel only very slightly tacky, and no residue should come off on your fingers.

3

2

3 Applying silver metal leaf

Lay a sheet of silver metal leaf on the glass by gently floating it onto the prepared surface. Completely cover the area with another piece, depending on the size of the glass, and tear small patches of leaf to cover any gaps. Gently brush the leaf onto the glass with a soft, dry brush, taking care not to let the brush touch any gaps where the gold size can make the brush sticky. Let the work dry before finally tidying up the flakes of leaf and raw edges. When the incense holders are completely dry, you can varnish them with gloss acrylic varnish to protect the silver leaf.

This mushroom-shaped glass

table lamp has a base and shade all in one, making it an especially interesting item that would look good used as a centerpiece. The electric fixtures can easily be removed before decorating, which makes it easier to work on, without wires and bulb holders getting in the way. The shape could have been treated in many different ways: for example with frosting

green swirl table lamp

medium in a simple graphic allover motif or with something more figurative using the same technique as the Sgraffito Leaf Vase (see page 40). I have given the piece a slightly retro feel, reflecting the design principles of the 1970s, with the use of three complementary shades of green. Choose an appropriate color scheme based on the room that it will be displayed in.

Try to keep a clean edge when painting over the masking plastic because any flaws will show up clearly when the lamp is lit. If you use a small soft-toned, preferably low-wattage bulb, it will cast a less harsh light.

you will need

Materials

Glass table lamp

Paper for templates

Masking tape

Pencil

Scissors

Self-adhesive plastic

Wide flat-headed ¾-inch paintbrush

Transparent glass paint in three shades
of green: aquamarine, bottle green,
and lime green

Techniques

Handpainting

Making the template

Making a template for a curved object, such as this lamp, takes several stages. Begin by wrapping a plain piece of paper part of the way around the glass and attach it with masking tape. Use a pencil to draw the shape of the top edge of the lamp and then sketch the lines for a curved shape that will be painted on the glass. The mask you will make will follow the curves of this shape, top and bottom, leaving a gap to be painted in greens. Build up the template piece by piece—you will be unable to get a smooth-fitting mask in one go.

1

Design hint:

• Use this masking technique to decorate the lamp in different ways—try gilding or use etching paste or frosting medium.

Painting on the design

Working with all three shades of green at the same time, start to paint the glass in long even strokes. Use a flat-headed brush with slightly stiff bristles, which will help the paint go on in lines. Merge the colors together at random as you are painting. Leave the paint to dry for several days before carefully removing the plastic mask.

Applying the mask

Using the paper guides, cut out the negative shapes in self-adhesive plastic and apply them to the lamp. Ease any air bubbles out of the plastic carefully; it is important with this design to stop any drips from seeping under the masking plastic.

While an allover design of small motifs would work very well on a plate, I wanted to try adding quite a lot of color to jazz up what was a rather dreary item in its undecorated state. This geometric design using large expanses of several different colors was perfect for a flat item where runs and drips were not going to cause many problems, and the squared shape of the plate would suit a more graphic approach.

To plan the design, I painted areas of plastic stationery sleeves and, when they were dry, cut them to shape. The pieces were laid on the plate and trimmed to size until I was happy with the overall balance of shapes before using masking tape as a guide for where to paint the blocks of color. This design was inspired by 1950s glassware, but I also decided to add some bold touches of black for texture and some additional black outliner as a part of the design itself rather than as it is normally used to outline motifs to prevent drips.

The final result has a dramatic visual impact, and the design could be duplicated, or varied as appropriate, for a whole set of plates.

geometric plate

you will need

Materials

Masking tape

Paper for masking and making
a template for outliner

Wide flat-headed ¾-inch paintbrush

Thin flat sponge for printing black
texture, such as a kitchen sponge

Transparent glass paints: red, orange,
aquamarine, olive green, and black

Scissors

Pencil

Black glass outliner

Techniques

Handpainting

Sponging (see page 20)

1a

1 Painting the transparent color blocks

Having planned the layout of the blocks of color, use
lengths of masking tape to define the position of
each square shape (1a). As is the case with many
projects, make sure you work on this design in
sections, leaving the paint to dry before masking out
the dried areas with paper to complete the next
rectangle of color. Take care not to apply masking
tape to areas already painted—it may lift off if it is
not absolutely dry. Use a wide flat-headed brush to
apply the paint in long even strokes; do not use too
much paint, but aim for fairly even coverage. If the
paint bleeds under the tape, it can be scraped off
with a craft knife later (1b).

1b

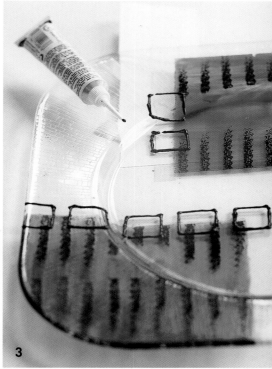

2

3

Sponging on the black stripes

As soon as the blocks of transparent color are quite dry, remove the masking tape and the paper, then pour a small amount of black glass paint into a small suitable container. Gently dip the sponge into the paint and carefully sponge stripes of black on top of the transparent color blocks. The end result will be a textured effect rather than a definite black line; the paint should be applied by using a gently rocking motion and the lines spaced evenly.

Using black outliner

Draw a row of about five simple squares on a piece of paper to use as a template. Tape the template to the underside of the plate and use it as a guide to apply a thin shape in black outliner. When you are planning the design, it helps if you apply the outliner to a piece of transparent plastic and cut it out when it is dry to place on top of the plate; this will help you decide where you want the squares to go. Let it dry for several days to allow the outliner to become completely hard.

This door panel is produced

very simply using glass etching spray on a plain panel. While having a house number etched commercially could be costly, this technique is inexpensive and can easily be adapted.

The spray is reasonably robust once it is completely dry and can be washed gently with soapy water. Nothing abrasive should be used however, and do not paint the outside surface of

etched door panel

the glass. If you are not happy with the finished work, you can scrub it off before the paint is dry using a pan scourer and denatured alcohol.

Remember to work in reverse, so house names and numbers should be looked at to check if they still look attractive back-to-front. If you do not need a house number but would prefer to use the idea as a means of providing more privacy, you could use simple motifs such as rows of the stationery dots (see Spray-etched Mirror, page 72) or enlarge typographic symbols such as exclamation marks, ampersands, asterisks, and symbols, which can look good when repeated.

you will need

Materials

Photocopy of house number, enlarged
    to suitable size

Pencil

Self-adhesive plastic

Cutting mat

Craft knife

Masking tape

Newspaper for masking

Glass etch spray

Carpenter's square

Craft knife for scraping away any
    mistakes

Techniques

Etching (see page 29 for a variation of
    the etching used here)

0 1
2 3
4 5
6 7
8 9

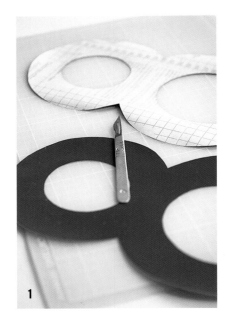

1

Making a template

Enlarge and photocopy the numerals for your house number to the required size using the templates supplied below. Cut them out to make a paper template for the etching. Draw around the templates on the backing paper of the plastic film, taking great care to reverse the numerals so they will be the right way around when they are seen from the outside of the glass. Then cut out the numerals.

2

3

Creating the design

Stick the paper template to the outside of the cleaned window with masking tape. A carpenter's square will help you keep the angles correct, and it can be taped to the glass while you are positioning the template and stencil. Now, working from the inside, use the masking tape to make a straight edge that will frame the design.

Applying the glass etch spray

Protect the remaining glass panel from the spray with newspaper, making sure there are no gaps, then carefully apply the self-adhesive plastic numerals, using the paper template as a guide. Carefully smooth the plastic down so the spray will not seep underneath. Shake the spray well before applying it to the glass in even sweeping movements. A thin layer will dry after a few minutes, and you can go over the glass a number of times to cover it evenly. This way you will avoid applying too much paint at once which could lead to drips and runs. The paint should be dry before you carefully peel off the plastic. Scrape away any paint that has seeped under the plastic with a craft knife.

This rectangular glass tank

is an example of "less is more." Only one side of the tank was painted because any more decoration would have overcrowded the design.

The straight sides of the tank suggested a simple, geometric treatment such as stripes, and a sponging technique was used to help soften the lines while avoiding the need for perfect edges. Use only a few basic colors for this design; the different

pink striped vase

shades of pink are achieved by mixing the colors together. Aim for two of the colors to be opaque paint (ceramic paint is perfect). Mix the paint on a small plastic tray—even grocery packaging. Microwave dinner trays are perfect for this task. They have the advantage of allowing you to have several colors on the go at once to be used for both sponging and handpainting.

To achieve the right balance of light and dark shades, you can plan your stripes on paper beforehand using colored crayons and use the sketch as a template if you prefer to have a more accurate guide from which to work.

you will need

Materials

Rectangular glass tank-shaped vase

Paper for template

Pencil

Scissors

Masking tape

Thin flat kitchen sponge

Transparent glass paints and opaque
   ceramic paints in a range of pink,
   red, and orange shades (see page 12)

No. 2 paintbrush

Techniques

Handpainting

Sponging (see page 20)

1 Making and positioning the template

Start by making a paper template. Draw a series of random vertical lines and tape the sketch inside the glass vase. Use the template as a guide to make the lines straight rather than as a rigid design plan. Then apply the template to the inside of the vase by securing it with small pieces of masking tape.

2 Applying transparent glass paint

Start by sponging on transparent glass paint with the edge of a thin flat piece of sponge. Include some very pale rose and make a wide stripe over which it will be possible to add some opaque color. Leave the work to dry at least overnight; if you apply more paint to wet paint the whole section can lift off.

1 & 2

Building up the design

Start to build up the design by sponging on some opaque ceramic paint. Mix the colors together with a paintbrush to get a good range of shades of pinkish reds. Sponge opaque paint on top of the pale transparent stripe, building up the design with different widths of stripes.

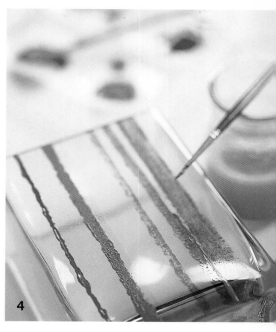

3

4

Using the paintbrush

It is important to use different widths of stripes in this design, so add some very thin stripes with a fine paintbrush. Use a stippling motion to give a bit of texture to the stripe to make it more like the sponged versions. Continue sponging and painting until you have a pleasing design, but avoid overworking the design and making it look too crowded.

Design hints:

• Multicolored candy stripes would give this vase a completely different look.

• Try using a range of different shades of blue for added impact.

Semiopaque ceramic paint

was used for this project instead of transparent glass paint, and yet the effect is light and airy, and surprisingly delicate. Don't be tempted to use more than three colors at a time or the design will look too busy, but experiment with other simple shapes and concentric patterns of dots such as circles, ovals, and triangles. You could decorate the handle or the rims of matching glasses with a simple row of dots worked as stripes horizontally or vertically around the shape. If you work fairly quickly, there is no reason why you should not experiment on the glassware itself; you will be able to wipe off the paint before it dries if necessary. This is sometimes a good approach when you are planning a design on a large object such as this pitcher, where testing ideas on a glass jar would not give enough idea of the scale.

Allow plenty of time for this project; you will have to work on it one section at a time, leaving the work to dry before turning to the next section. Also, the dots need enough paint to make them slightly raised to show up well.

dotted pitcher

you will need

Materials

Paper for templates

Pencil

Scissors

Masking tape

No. 2 paintbrush

Ceramic paints in soft, complementary
    colors: soft green, plum, and
    French navy

Techniques

Handpainting

1 Planning the design

The first stage is to clean the glass to remove all traces of grease and dirt, and then dry it thoroughly. Draw and cut out three differently sized and proportioned paper rectangles, which will be used as templates, and stick them to the inside of the pitcher with masking tape. Arrange them so you have an even balance of the three shapes. Simply work freestyle until you have a pleasing and balanced arrangement.

1

2

Design hint:
• Try varying the colors and proximity of dots within the concentric circles and squares.

Applying the dots

Using the fine paintbrush, work using the template as a guide to create dots of paint around the outer edge of the shape. Practice will tell you how much paint to apply, but you are aiming for a slightly raised dot of paint, although not thick enough to cause the paint to run. Rest the pitcher in the reel of masking tape to support it at an angle as you work. Plan the colors to work in a system so that, for instance, all the largest shapes are painted in the same sequence of colors. When the outer line of dots is nearly dry, you can work on the next row. There are three concentric rows of dots for each motif. You can work freestyle or, if you prefer, draw the lines on each template as a guide.

Wall mirrors are an elegant

way of bringing reflected light into a room where you want to avoid having too much clutter on the walls. With strategic positioning, a mirror can transform a dark room into one that appears light and airy.

Simple geometric designs can be achieved quickly by using glass etching spray and stationery dots. These are available in a variety of shapes and sizes, and provide a good clean edge. They are much simpler to use than having to cut out a lot of dots accurately by hand.

When using spray paint of any kind, there's always a danger that paint may seep under the masking paper or tape, so try to get a good seal on the edges and avoid spraying on a thick layer at one time. Repositionable spray adhesive can help stick the mask down temporarily, so use it if possible. The glass etch spray is reasonably durable, but in the way of any paint effect, care must be taken not to scratch the surface with abrasives when cleaning.

spray-etched mirror

you will need

Materials

Large round wall mirror

Masking tape and paper for masking

Self-adhesive dots from an office supply
   store

Glass etch spray

Carpenter's square

Craft knife for scraping away any
   mistakes

Techniques

Etching (see page 29 for a variation of
   the etching used here)

1

Planning the design

Sketch some rough ideas for the mirror; then plan your design with pieces of plain paper, working directly on the mirror to get the right idea of scale. When you are happy with the placement, use plain white paper to mask off the sections that will not be treated. Use the carpenter's square to make accurate angles. Stick the paper down with masking tape very firmly, arranging overlapping pieces if necessary, but taking great care that no spray will be able to get under the paper. You can put some weights on the edge of the masking to help prevent this when you are ready to spray. Use a carpenter's square to help you line up the position for the adhesive dots. Stick them down accurately and firmly to avoid seepage while spraying.

Cleaning up the design

Remove the mask before the paint is absolutely dry so you can clean any edges if necessary by scraping with a knife. You can also clean small mistakes with a cotton swab dipped in lighter fluid or denatured alcohol.

3

Spraying on the glass etch spray

Shake the can of glass etch spray for several seconds. Then, holding it above the mirror at a distance of about 10-12 inch, spray in a gentle sweeping movement. It is better to repeat with several layers of spray rather than one heavy coat to eliminate the chance of drips and runs. Work in a well-ventilated area.

With their colorful fish motifs, these delightful canisters will look great in a bathroom setting. Alter the colors to suit your chosen scheme and display them to create an eye-catching feature.

The motifs are created using a combination of techniques such as handpainting, monoprinting, and sgraffito, and this is perfect for more intricate figurative designs. The steps are shown here just

fish canisters

on the lid of the canister to make the details clearer, but the method is exactly the same for the body of the canister.

These storage jars could be used for food, stationery, or sewing notions, and the motifs can be adapted accordingly. You could choose pasta shells, paper clips, or buttons instead of the fish design illustrated here. Look for unusually shaped glassware that will instantly give your jar collection added interest. Make sure the lids are noncorrodible, especially if you are planning to use storage jars in the bathroom or kitchen.

you will need

Materials

Glass storage canisters with lids

Paper or cardboard for making
   templates

Pencil

Scissors for cutting out templates

Masking tape

Paper towels

No. 2 paintbrush

Opaque ceramic paint to match the
   glass paints

Black glass outliner

Transparent glass paints: aquamarine,
   orange, violet, and lime green

Fine-pointed scissors or large needle
   inserted into a cork for sgraffito

Techniques

Handpainting

Monoprinting (see page 24)

Sgraffito (see page 29)

Designing the fish motif

Draw and cut out a fish template several times and tape the motif to the inside of the glass to mark where you want to paint the designs. Draw the outline of the fish on a small piece of paper towel, then paint the outline with opaque ceramic paint directly onto the paper towel using a No. 2 paintbrush. Make sure there is enough paint on the paper to allow it to transfer onto the glass, but not enough to cause it to bleed or make blobs. Carefully place the paper on the glass without smudging it and gently press the design from the back of the paper onto the glass. Lift the paper towel away cleanly in one movement, but don't worry if you smudge it slightly since this can be scraped away later. If you have any gaps left, you can fill them in with a paintbrush. When the outline is dry, paint the inside of the motif with transparent glass paint and let it dry for a few hours.

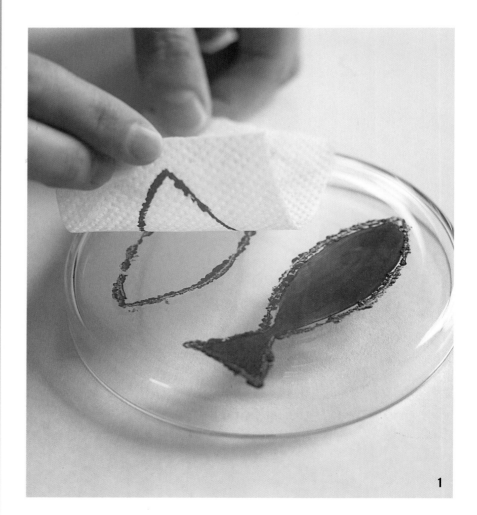

1

Design hints:
- Experiment with various ceramic outliners available in different colors.
- Vary the design and simplify the motif by omitting the scratched detail.

3

Outlining in black

Using black outliner, apply dots of paint over the transparent paints. Work by eye rather than worrying about being too accurate since the spontaneity will enhance the overall effect. Place a dot on the face for the eye.

Adding the detail

Complete the design on the fish by scratching a circle around the eye and lines along the body and tail with the point of the scissors or, if you prefer, a needle inserted into a cork. Brush away the flakes of paint as you work.

Decorating glassware with

mosaic means that the effect can be seen from both sides. The bowl used here was made from pressed glass with a texture of close concentric circles, and this design complements the three-dimensional effect of the mosaic beautifully.

I chose an offbeat selection of colors from a large bag of mixed mosaic tiles that contained some with a metallic gold tint as well as the more usual opalescent glass, and included some greens to harmonize with the slightly greenish tint of the glass bowl. You can also buy sheets of single-color mosaic tiles quite inexpensively, although they cannot be purchased in small quantities so you will have a lot left over. However, once you have discovered how easy it is to work in mosaic, you will no doubt be drawn to undertaking more projects of this kind.

The gel medium used here was transparent, but you could also try using soft opalescent shades for embedding the mosaic to fit in with the colors within the design. The gel has the advantage of being extremely durable, so it is perfect for the more robust embedding technique of mosaic.

mosaic bowl

you will need

Materials

Large glass bowl

Porcelain marker

Transparent gel medium

Applicator bottle with long narrow
	nozzle for the gel medium (optional)

Assorted mosaic pieces in about 4–6
	different complementary colors

Mosaic cutters or tile cutters

Techniques

Embedding (see page 26)

1 Drawing guidelines for gel medium

Use the porcelain marker on the reverse side of the glass to draw two parallel lines about ¾ inch apart around the edge of the bowl to guide you when applying the gel medium.

2 Applying the gel medium

The gel medium can run if too much is done at one time, so rest the bowl at an angle on a roll of masking tape. If you are using an applicator bottle, fill it with gel medium. Gently squeeze gel along the two lines you have drawn; fill in between them with a zigzag squiggle.

3a

Embedding the mosaic

Cut the mosaic tiles into smaller pieces with the cutters or tile snips. Work with the tool inside a plastic bag to prevent shards from flying off—the mosaic glass can be sharp (3a). Now gently press the mosaic chips into the wet gel medium (3b). Avoid any pieces with sharp edges. Let the section dry before turning the bowl around to work on the next section. When the work is complete, go over the mosaic with a little more gel, filling in any gaps where the edges of the mosaic may not be fully embedded.

3b

Candle holders and votive

glasses are small and easy to handle, so this is a good project to try out embedding techniques. Seed and pearl beads give the votive candles a pretty, delicate appeal that looks luxurious and exotic. There is tremendous scope for experimenting with color on this project, but choose your selection of beads in complementary colors, mixing sizes and shapes in a range of similar shades. Include some bugle beads, which are perfect for linear designs such as the holder shown here, and look out for pearl beads with slight tints as well as the classic ivory. Using pearlized paint to cover the glass makes an effective background, but you could use clear glass or combine embedding beads on silver-gilded glass for a more opulent effect.

Votive candles are a safe way of softly lighting a room with candles. Another idea is to fill decorated glasses with candle sand or stand tapers in tiny pebbles as I did with the Gilded Incense Holders (see page 48). As with all candles, make sure you do not leave them unattended while they are burning.

embedded votives

you will need

Materials

Small drinking glasses or
   purpose-made votive holders

Sponge for applying paint

Scissors

Pearlized glass or ceramic paint—or
   add pearlized medium to colored
   paint to achieve pearlized effect

Paper for template

Pencil

Thick gel medium for glass painting
   for embedding the circular design
   in a color to complement the beads
   such as opalescent pink

Pearlized or silver metallic outliner
   for embedding the beads

Flat-headed ¾ inch paintbrush

Selection of glass beads such as seed
   beads, pearl beads, and bugle beads

Long darning needle embedded in a cork
   to help pick up and position beads

Silver outliner paste

Techniques

Sponging (see page 20)

Embedding (see page 26)

1 Sponging on the frosting

Mix together the pearlized medium and the transparent glass paint
to make a pearlized frosting. I used a water-based paint for this project.
Sponge the glass all over with the paint. Cover completely, including the
base. You can paint the base a slightly darker shade as I did for the
incense holders to give the color more depth.

1

Positioning the seed and pearl beads

To make the medallion-shaped beaded motif, draw a circle template on paper and tape it inside the glass. Squeeze a generous amount of gel medium onto the shape, using the flat edge of a paintbrush to help achieve a roughly circular shape. To embed the beads, put a selection of seed and pearl beads in the gel, using the tip of the needle to ease them into position. Leave to dry at least overnight, lying flat, because the gel can easily fall off in one piece if you are not careful.

Outlining with bugle beads

Pipe a thin line of silver outliner around the edge of the circle and, while it is still wet, put bugle beads in the paste to encircle the whole medallion. You can add more layers around the edge of the motif, depending on the size and scale of the glassware.

The circular motifs within this

tabletop could not be simpler, and yet the effect is attractive and contemporary. The table legs were black, and were given a coat of matte silver spray paint to lighten the whole look of the table.

There is no need to be precise about cutting out perfect shapes; the design works well with circles drawn freehand and cut out with scissors. I used a round design, but this could be adapted

circular glass tabletop

for a square or rectangular-shaped tabletop with irregular-sized squares or rectangles. If you have difficulty with the plastic film rolling as you try to cut it, try partially rolling the area you are not cutting out and securing this tube shape with masking tape which leaves a smaller area free to work on. When you have completed this area, remove the masking tape and roll up the area you have prepared: the tube formed helps keep the work area flatter.

When using glass etching spray, do not apply too many coats, or the frosting effect will be lost and the circles will look very white.

you will need

Materials

Circular glass tabletop

Pencil

Self-adhesive plastic

Fine-pointed scissors (or craft knife
used on a cutting mat)

Masking tape and newspaper

Glass etching spray

No. 2 paintbrush

Orange transparent glass paint

Techniques

Etching (see page 29 for a variation of
this technique)

1

1 Drawing the circles

Draw a circle on a piece of self-adhesive plastic the size of the area you
wish to decorate. This will depend on the size of the tabletop; I drew
around a small plate. Now fill the circle with a series of smaller circles of
different sizes. You can draw them freehand or use bottle tops, small
glasses, coins, or other suitable items as templates. Cut out the small
circles very neatly using scissors, or use a craft knife if you prefer.

Positioning the design

Using the plate you drew around placed under the glass to guide you, position the plastic film and remove the backing paper. Mask the remaining exposed edges with newspaper and masking tape. Fill the centers of the circles with smaller circles cut from the plastic film. Carefully rub the stencil to eliminate all air bubbles.

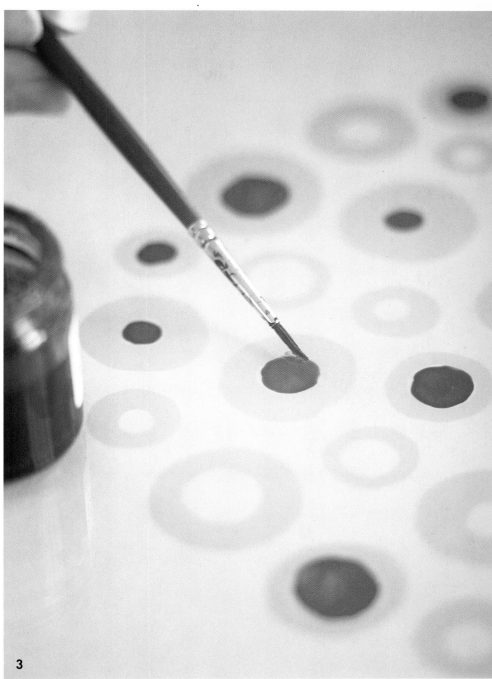

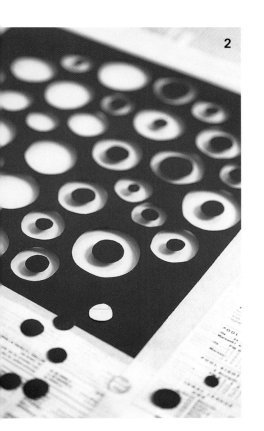

Coloring the tabletop

Spray the stuck-down design evenly with the glass etching spray. Leave the glass to dry completely before carefully removing the masking stencil. Paint some of the centers of the frosted dots with some transparent glass paint and leave the remaining dots without paint. When the paint has dried, turn the glass over and place it in position on the table legs. This means that the reverse side will be in use and the painted surface will be protected from scratching. Because of the larger scale of this project and the use of the glass etching spray, it is not suitable to use paints that require oven baking.

index

Page numbers in **bold** refer to the projects; illustrations are indicated in *italic*

a

acrylic gilding medium *22*
adhesive, repositionable 72
alcohol, cleaning with 15, 19

b

beads:
    embedded votives **84–7**
    embedding 26–8, *26–8*
bowl, mosaic **80–3**
bristle brushes 14–15
brushes:
    cleaning 13
    types of 14–15
brushmarks 14
bugle beads 84, *87*

c

candle holders, embedded **84–7**
canisters, fish **76–9**
ceramic paint 13
    dotted pitcher **68–71**
    fish canisters **76–9**
    gilded incense holders **50–1**
    monoprinting with *25*
    pink striped vase **64–7**
checks, sponging *21*
circular glass tabletop **88–91**
cleaners, solvent-based 15
colored glass 10
colors, mixing 19
craft knife, correcting mistakes 19, *75*
curved objects, templates for 54
cutting:
    mosaic tiles *83*
    self-adhesive plastic 89

d

denatured alcohol, correcting
    mistakes with 75
design 16–17
door panel, etched **60–3**
dotted pitcher **68–71**
drips 19

e

embedding 26–8, *26–8*
    mosaic bowl **80–3**
    votives **84–7**
enlarging motifs 17
etching 29
    circular glass tabletop **88–91**
    door panel **60–3**
    hoarfrost shelf **44–7**
    spray-etched mirror **72–5**

f

felt-tip pens 13, 19
fine-pointed brushes 14
fish canisters **76–9**
frames, frosted **36–9**
frosting:
    embedded votives *86*
    frosted picture frames **36–9**

g

gel medium 13
    embedded votives **84–7**
    mosaic bowl **80–3**
geometric plate **56–9**
gilding 22, *22–3*
    incense holders **48–51**
glass jewels, embedding 26
glass paint 13
    circular glass tabletop **88–91**
    fish canisters **76–9**
    frosted picture frames **36–9**
    geometric plate **56–9**
    gilded incense holders **50–1**
    green swirl table lamp **52–5**
    pink striped vase **64–7**
    purple sponged glasses **32–5**
        techniques 19

glasses, purple sponged 32-35
glassware 10
gold size 22
    gilded incense holders **50–1**
green swirl table lamp **52–5**

h

handpainting:
    dotted pitcher **68–71**
    fish canisters **76–9**
    frosted picture frames **36–9**
    geometric plate **56–9**
    green swirl table lamp **54–5**
    pink striped vase **64–7**
hoarfrost shelf **44–7**

i

incense holders, gilded **48–51**

l

lamp, green swirl **52–5**
leaf vase, sgraffito **40–3**
lighter fluid, correcting mistakes with
    75

m

marker, porcelain *82*
masking:
    etched door panel 63
    frosted picture frames 38
    geometric plate 58–9
    spray-etched mirror 74–5
masking tape 15
    paint seeping under 19, 72
materials 14–15
metal leaf:
    gilded incense holders **48–51**
    techniques 22, *23*
mirror, spray-etched **72–5**
mistakes, correcting 19, 75
monoprinting 17, *24–5*, 25
    fish canisters **76–9**
mosaic tiles:
    bowl **80–3**
    cutting *83*
    embedding 26

motifs:
  circles *88, 89, 90–1*
  dots, *68, 69, 70–1, 72, 73–5*
  enlarging or reducing 17
  fish *76–9*
  geometric 56, *57–9, 72, 73–5*
  leaves 42
  numbers, *60, 61, 62–3*
  stripes 64, *65–7*

n
needles, sgraffito 29
numbers, etched door panel **60-3**

o
outliner 13, 16–17
  embedding techniques *27*
  fish canisters **78-9**
  geometric plate **56-9**
  monoprinting with *24–5, 25*

p
painting *see* handpainting
paints 13
  see also ceramic paint; glass paint;
    pearlized paint
palettes 19
paper towels 19
  monoprinting with *25*
pearl beads, embedded votives **84-7**
pearlized paint 19
  embedded votives **84-7**
  embedding techniques *27, 28*
  gilded incense holders **50-1**
pens, felt-tip 13, 19
photocopiers, enlarging motifs 17
picture frames, frosted **36-9**
pink striped vase **64-7**
pitcher, dotted **68-71**
plastic, self-adhesive *see* self-adhesive
  plastic
plate, geometric **56-9**
porcelain marker *82*
purple sponged glasses **32-5**

r
reducing motifs 17
relief outliner *see* outliner
runs 19

s
scissors, sgraffito 29
seed beads:
  embedded votives **84-7**
  embedding techniques *26–8, 26–8*
self-adhesive plastic 15
  cutting 89
  etched door panel **62-3**
  green swirl table lamp **54-5**
  hoarfrost shelf **46-7**
sgraffito 29
  fish canisters **76-9**
  leaf vase **40-3**
shelf, hoarfrost **44-7**
silver metal leaf *23*
  gilded incense holders **48-51**
silver outliner paste 86
size, gilding 22
solvent-based cleaners 15
solvent-based paint 13
  techniques 19
sponges 14
sponging 21, *21*
  cutting stamps 34
  embedded votives **84-7**
  embedding technique *28*
  frosted picture frames **36-9**
  geometric plate **56-9**
  gilded incense holders **50-1**
  pink striped vase **64-7**
  purple sponged glasses **32-5**
spray-etched mirror **72-5**
stencils:
  cutting 15
  etching 29
  paint running under 19

storage jars, fish **76-9**
stripes:
  pink striped vase **64-7**
  sponging *21*

t
table lamp, green swirl **52-5**
tabletop, circular glass **88-91**
techniques 18–29
templates:
  for curved objects 54
  gilding technique *22*
textured glass 10
three-dimensional sponging *21*
transfer leaf, gilding 22, *23*
transparent glass paint *see* glass paint
tumblers, purple sponged **32-5**

u
utility knife, *see* craft knife

v
varnish 19
  gilding technique *22*
vases:
  pink striped vase **64-7**
  sgraffito leaf vase **40-3**
votives, embedded **84-87**

w
water-based paint 13
  embedded votives *86*
  embedding technique 26, *26–7*

suppliers

Aaron Brothers

(888) 532-9372

1270 S. Goodrich Blvd.

Commerce, CA 90022

www.aaronbrothers.com

Artcity.com

(866) ARTCITY

1350 Kelton Ave., Ste.308

Los Angeles, CA 90024

www.artcity.com

Art Supply Warehouse

(800) 995-6778

5325 Departure Dr.

Raleigh, NC 27616

www.aswexpress.com

Jo-Ann Fabric & Crafts

(800) 525-4951

5555 Darrow Rd.

Hudson, OH 44236

www.joann.com

Michaels Stores Inc.

(800) Michaels

8000 Bent Branch Drive

Irving TX 75063

www.michaels.com

MisterArt.com

(800) 423-7382

1800 Peachtree St. NW, Ste. 250

Atlanta, GA 30309

www.misterart.com

acknowledgments

Many thanks to Emma, Carl, Nicky, Isabel, and Sandra for all their help and advice and for making working with them such a pleasure.

First published in the United States by **Laurel Glen Publishing**

An imprint of the Advantage Publishers Group

5880 Oberlin Drive

San Diego, CA 92121-4794

www.advantagebooksonline.com

First published in 2001 by Conran Octopus Limited

North American Edition

Publisher Allen Orso

Imprint Manager Rachel Petrella

Managing Editor JoAnn Padgett

Development Mgr. Elizabeth McNulty

Project Editor Bobby Wong

Assistant Editor Mana Monzavi

ISBN 1-57145-519-1

Library of Congress Cataloging-in-Publication Data available upon request.

Printed in China

1 2 3 4 5   01 02 03 04 05